herbert bayer: photographic works

montecito, california, 1977

herbert bayer: photographic works

an exhibition organized by
arco center for visual art
los angeles, california
19 april — 28 may 1977

introduction by leland rice
essay by beaumont newhall

ARCO
CENTER
FOR
VISUAL
ART

Cover: *In Search of Times Past,* 1959
     Photomontage
     9¼ x 13⅜ in.
     23.5 x 32.0 cm.

In all measurements, height precedes width

All camera images are modern prints from
original negatives unless otherwise
indicated by an asterisk.

contents

acknowledgments

The art of Herbert Bayer — his paintings, sculpture, graphics, typography, environmental design, exhibition design — are well-known contributions to twentieth century art. His photomontages and fotoplastiken are important to the vision of many present-day photographers, yet his camera images have rarely been seen. In the two years that I have known Herbert Bayer, I have come to realize that there should be documentation of his photographic work. This exhibition and catalog will mark the first comprehensive viewing in this country of this material.

This project has received the support of many people and many have been involved in its organization. I want to record deepest thanks and gratitude to Leland Rice who co-directed the exhibition with me, and whose knowledge, curiosity and patience led the rest of us. Lilli Cristin, who designed the catalog with the cooperation of Herbert Bayer, was also helpful in editing the book: and beyond that, her graciousness, humour, and sensitive insights into the material played an impressive role in seeing this book to its fruition. I would also like to thank Steven Yates, research assistant, who researched and prepared the photographic bibliography. And to Beaumont Newhall, who took time from his busy schedule to write the essay on Bayer for this catalog, I extend my most sincere appreciation.

Within the staff of the ARCO Center for Visual Art, Fritz Frauchiger, assistant to the director, was an invaluable source of help in the organization of the material used in the exhibition and catalog. Sique Kuchta, gallery assistant, efficiently aided in numerous details throughout the planning of the exhibition and catalog.

Leland Rice and I made many trips to Montecito to confer with Bayer. Those early morning drives along the Pacific Coast were filled with great expectations. And on our return trips, usually in the evening, we were always more elated about our project than we had been the time before. Herbert Bayer had made the day exciting and shared his energies and enthusiasms with us. He is a gentleman of extraordinary charm. I want to thank him for the opportunity to work with him on this exhibition.

betty gold, *director*
arco center for visual art

6

introduction

The chaotic climate of the early 1920's post-World War I period was replaced in the mid-twenties with an irrepressible optimism centered in the liberating potential of scientific and technological achievement. An unbounded enthusiasm was focused on the new inventions that this technology created. There was a tendency to glorify the engineering feats of the day like the airplane and monumental urban architecture. One of the primary attractions at this time was the introduction of the miniature hand-camera. With the newfound flexibility of such an instrument, mechanical perfection was within reach of everyone. This allowed for a startling amount of "new" imagery to emerge, not surprisingly rooted simultaneously in scientific theory and intellectual thought.

The camera, as a creative tool, allowed the visual imagination of the artist to flow freely into areas hitherto unexplored. Fascination with capturing optically the plasticity of both organic and geometric forms created unusual relationships of familiar subjects. The tradition of linear perspective could be rendered perfectly or lens distortion could purposely exaggerate the reality of perspective. What evolved during this rich period of photographic exploration was a pronounced concern for a greater awareness of the appearance of things.

It was during this period that photography gained importance for the Bauhaus artist, Herbert Bayer, and began to influence his work. He had inventively used photographic images in designing numerous posters and book covers, most notedly the typography exhibition poster for Kandinsky in 1926. But it wasn't until he moved to Berlin in 1928 to set up private practice as an artist and designer of typography as well as to continue his painting, that he began a concentrated body of work in this medium.

In an accompanying essay by Beaumont Newhall, Bayer's career at the Bauhaus and his multi-uses of photography are discussed at length. Our concern here is to take a close look at the methodology he employed in his camera work and the later use of the photograph as a collage element.

Bayer's camera vision and imaginative approach to composition partially took rise from the art movement, constructivism, as well as the reasoned and conscious teachings of the Bauhaus. An early interest in how the preciseness of the camera recorded fundamental geometric forms like the circle and axis were central concerns. Strong uses of diagonal shapes that cut across many of his pictures' open spaces in combination with exaggerated camera vantage points produced a new order of object relationships. Symmetry was neither sought nor avoided, but was determined by the innate balance of the individual objects before the camera lens (Nos. 5, 9, 11). The arrangements of animate and inanimate subjects as photographed by Bayer are not accidental or arbitrary. The criss-cross structure of the iron support systems on the suspension bridge in Marseilles is a brilliant example of the way he organized the picture plane (Nos. 4, 9, 10). To quote Bayer, "Fixed and flexible parts seem to be alive in their connection . . . like a fantasy of wire and air."[1]

The abstract nature of light through the effects of cast shadows and raking sunlight heightened the artist's awareness of how light and dark values could compositionally extend common vision. Not only were the accustomed frontal and profile views used, but the newfound excitement of the view from above, commonly referred to as the bird's-eye view, and that from below, the frog's-eye view, acted to dissolve the traditional vanishing point perspective, shifting it to any number of possible positions. The varied foreshortening that took place as camera position was changed caused familiar forms to reveal their unfamiliar fragments. Given this information it becomes understandable to some degree why two photographers like Bayer and Moholy-Nagy might happen upon the same subject, the boats in the harbor, and treat it compositionally in similar ways. This can be attributed partly to the mutual popularity of the subject matter, but even more so to the widespread common visual sensibilities practiced at the time. This mutualness of attitude is further substantiated in what Bayer says about the use of the camera: "It reproduces in general, without essential personal interlineations, the appearance of an object."[2]

The principle of inversion, long applied to weaving, offered still another approach. And that was the complete altering of the tonal range of a photograph by printing a negative impression of the image rather than the standard positive one. All the light and dark values were reversed, causing the resulting linear areas of white in the print to become very active, dynamically delineating the forms of the whole picture (Nos. 14, 15). This is unique in the pictorial arts to the medium of photography.

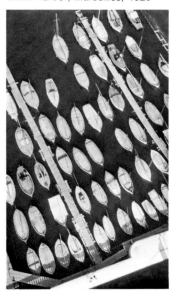

Small Harbor, Marseilles, 1928

Bayer began working with the technique of photomontage as early as 1929. During the twenties there was a widespread use of methods of collage which had directly come about out of a need the art community felt for combining new materials to make a more relevant modernist statement. Through this method of working, Bayer would cut up photos, reassemble them, paste them down on top of each other, sometimes retouch, and finally rephotograph the preliminary art work to arrive at the end product. This way of working offered a relatively independent use of pictures of a diverse origin, nature, and proportion, eliciting combinations that expressed specific ideas. Fragments of reality were formally simplified through this technique, presenting images that

postulated a kind of science fiction of the mind. Photomontage lent itself to an increasing intellectualization as evidenced in this quote: "We live in a time of the greatest precision and of maximum contrasts: photomontage offers us a means to express this. It shows ideas: photography shows objects."[3]

In *Profil en Face* (No. 54), we see a close parallel to a series of Bayer's watercolors, most notedly ones that experimented with the relationships between form and perspective. The use of reversal letters with their cast shadows flattened against planes of geometric forms in *World of Letters* can be compared with the method of cutting up and arrangement of the letter R and the cubistically profiled faces in this early photomontage. The static singular viewpoint gave way to a dynamic multi-point of view concept and additionally, as Bayer points out, ". . . the montage makes images of a surreal character, of the impossible and the invisible possible. It has been compared to a conquest of the irrational, it can express the hallucinations of dreams."[4] This body of work was intended to be a part of a "picture story" project about dreams and man, to be created separately and organized later as the material naturally evolved. It was never completed.

The term photoplastics or *Fotoplastiken*, the latter term being used by Bayer, was originally coined by Moholy-Nagy to stand for a method of "simultaneous presentations" of a heterogeneous selection of materials. In constructing the images in this series, Bayer would set up the objects, many being handmade by the artist himself, in his studio by propping them up, sometimes with string. Then, after photographing the arrangement from a number of camera positions for maximum effect, he would touch out the visible supporting props he didn't want to leave showing with an airbrushing technique. In a number of the pieces he further used airbrushing to add clouds which realistically appeared as if to be floating in and about the arranged objects. This retouched preliminary art work would then be photographed and a standard print made from the negative. With this technique Bayer was able to depict organic and geometric plastic objects in an innovative relationship between nature and imaginary environments. The cut-out photographs that were sometimes used were shaped to echo and relate to a sense of visual depth and reality (Nos. 67, 72).

In contrasting Bayer's methods with Moholy we see at least two significant differences. In the case of Moholy, he drew directly upon the photographic image or connected the cut-up photograph by drawing in lines and shapes that acted to homogenize the whole picture. Therefore, Moholy formed his images by collaging a number of photographs together while Bayer worked from a specific still life set-up in his studio, adding handwork later. Bayer then re-photographed his art work to arrive at the final image; Moholy usually didn't.

Bayer's *Fotoplastiken* were all done in 1936 except for one, *Hands Act* (No. 65), which was first intended as a photomontage but later placed in the *plastiken* series because of the very sculptured nature in the positioning of the hands. In 1936 Bayer decided to publish both series in small editions of five or six sets, each including ten images. These sets were primarily given away to close artist friends. In both editions, the original photographic prints measured somewhere between 11 by 15 inches and 12 by 16 inches and were printed on a heavy double-weight mat paper with a warm tone scale. These same images were recently reprinted in 1968 in an edition of forty under the supervision of Bayer, and the pictures measured approximately 10 by 13½ inches. In addition to notating the existence of these two sets of the photomontages and *Fotoplastiken*, it should also be mentioned that while selecting the work for this exhibition we discovered still

Moholy-Nagy, *Boats at Marseilles Harbor*, 1929

other prints of these images made in the intervening years.

It was our desire to display, when possible, the original print in order to capture the characteristics of the early papers' range of tones and general appearance as they differ substantially from contemporary impressions. All of the photomontages and *Fotoplastiken* in the exhibition are original prints. In the case of the camera images, the vast majority are contemporary prints made in 1976 from the original negative. The 14 vintage camera images we are showing vary in size from 5 by 9 inches to 9 by 14 inches. This exhibition of Herbert Bayer's photographic works concentrates on the period between the time he left the Bauhaus, 1928, to settle in Berlin, to his immigration to the United States in 1938. In his long and distinguished career as an artist and designer, it seems only natural that we should now focus on his photography activity as one more link to connecting the varied facets of his art.

leland rice

Footnotes

1. Herbert Bayer. *Die Schwebefähre von Marseille*. Germany: *Das Illustrierte Blatt*, No. 49, 1929, unpaged.

2. Herbert Bayer. *Werbephoto*. Germany: *Wirtschaft: Lichkeit*, February 1928, unpaged.

3. Cesar Domela-Nieuwenhuis. Translated from the introduction to catalog of the Exhibition Fotomontage, held at the Kunstgewerbemuseum, Berlin 1931, pp. 5, 6.

4. Herbert Bayer. Speech to the German Photographic Society, 1969.

biography

1900. Born in Haag, Austria.
1919. Apprenticed in architect
George Schmidthammer's studio for
architecture and decorative arts, Linz.
1920. Assistant to architect
Emanuel Margold, Darmstadt; primarily
concerned with graphic design
and typography.
1921-23. Enrolled in Bauhaus, Weimar,
studied mural painting under Kandinsky.
Created "universal" alphabet.
1925-28. Master at Bauhaus, Dessau.
Taught typography and advertising layout.
1928-38. Berlin. Painting, photography,
graphic design, exhibition architecture.
Director of Dorland studio and (1929-1930)
art director of *Vogue*.
1930. Co-designed exhibition "Deutscher
Werkbund," Grand Palais, Paris (with
Walter Gropius, Laszlo Moholy-Nagy,
Marcel Breuer). First prize award in the first
comprehensive exhibition of foreign
advertising photography.
1931. Designed exhibition
"Baugewerkschaften," Berlin (with
Walter Gropius, Laszlo Moholy-Nagy).
1938-46. New York. Painting, sculpture,
architecture, environmental design.
1938. Designed exhibition "Bauhaus
1919-1928," The Museum of Modern Art,
New York and (with Ise and Walter Gropius)
edited the catalog *Bauhaus 1919-1928*.
1942. Designed exhibition "Road to Victory"
(directed by Edward Steichen), The
Museum of Modern Art, New York.
1943. Designed exhibition "Airways to
Peace," The Museum of Modern Art,
New York.
1945. Director of art and design, Dorland
International. Designed exhibition "Art in
Industry," Art Institute of Chicago.
1946-76. Aspen, Colorado. Painting,
exhibition design, graphic design. Design
consultant for the development of Aspen.
Consultant and architect for Aspen Institute
for Humanistic Studies.
1946-67. Design consultant and, from 1956,
chairman of the department of design,
Container Corporation of America; designed
office buildings and factories. Art director of
"Great Ideas of Western Man."
1948-53. Edited and designed *World
Geo-graphic Atlas*.
1966- . Art and design consultant for
Atlantic Richfield Company.
1967-71. Designed exhibition "50 Years
Bauhaus," Wurttembergischer Kunstverein,
Stuttgart; Royal Academy of Art, London;
Illinois Institute of Technology, Chicago; Art
Gallery of Ontario, Toronto; Pasadena Art
Museum, Pasadena; Museo de Arte
Moderno, Buenos Aires; National Museum
of Modern Art, Tokyo.
1968. "Articulated Wall," highway sculpture
on Route of Friendship between Mexico
City and Azteca Stadium, commissioned for
the Olympic Games.
1968-74. Designed tapestries, wall
hangings and carpets, murals, fountains
and sculpture for Atlantic Richfield
Company offices in Chicago, New York,
Los Angeles and Philadelphia. Project for
beautification of Atlantic Richfield Company
refinery, Philadelphia.
1969. Kulturpreis, Koln.
1972-73. "Double Ascension" for ARCO
Plaza, Los Angeles.
1973. Elected fellow, Aspen Institute for
Humanistic Studies, Doctor Honoris Causa,
Technische, Hochschule, Graz.
1973-74. Designed Anderson Park,
Aspen Institute.
1974. Doctor of Fine Arts, honorary degree,
Philadelphia College of Art. Designed
interior of Aspen Institute, Berlin.
Co-architect of Boettcher building,
Aspen Institute.
1975. Honorary fellow, Royal Academy of
Fine Arts, the Hague. Moved to
Montecito, California.

herbert bayer and photography

In the early years of the 1920s, there was little if any interest in photography as a creative art form on the part of the European avant garde art world. It is true that the German Dada group — in particular George Grosz, John Heartfield, Hannah Höch and Raoul Hausmann — was making use of photographs clipped from magazines and newspapers in montages when the 1920 Berlin Dada Messe was dominated by their work, and that in Geneva in 1918 Christian Schad was making those cameraless "Schadographs" which preceded the "Rayographs" of Man Ray and the "photograms" of Laszlo Moholy-Nagy. But German photographers, so far as we can judge from reproductions in camera magazines and exhibition catalogs, were still attuned to the impressionistic, painterly style of the 1900s.

None of the vigor of Alfred Stieglitz's uncompromising "straight" photographs that so shocked the art world of New York when he exhibited them in 1921 was known in Germany. Nor was there anything being done comparable to the abstract "Vortographs" of Alvin Langdon Coburn of 1917, nor the bold experiments in the simplification of form and emphasis of texture and structure to be seen in the photographs of Charles Sheeler and Paul Strand in America, of Malcolm Arbuthnot in England and Pierre Dubreuil in France — all predating 1921. Indeed, as late as 1926, an exhibition billed in Frankfurt as the first large-scale exhibition of German photography since World War I, showed the weakest backwash of the pictorial movement of the turn of the century — soft focus, sentimental landscapes and village scenes — in spite of the fact that the posters were bold graphic designs, mirroring the new typography.

But by 1929 Germany had become the world champion of what was then called "the new photography." The art world was now deeply interested in photography. Such periodicals as *Die Form, Das Kunstblatt,* and *Cahiers d'Art* regularly published photographs and articles about the medium. The Bauhaus, a highly successful experimental art school in Weimar, and later Dessau, which sought to create a union between art and technology, published *Painting, Photography, Film* by Laszlo Moholy-Nagy in 1925; it was popular enough to be followed by a second edition in 1927. Form, created by and through photography was its theme: together with his own photograms and photographs taken from above and below, negative prints, double exposures and photomontages, Moholy-Nagy included photographs made for scientific purposes and for the daily press. *Es kommt der neue Fotograf!* ("Here Comes the New Photographer") by Werner Graeff, a handbook urging the abandonment of conventional rules of composition and perspective, appeared in 1929.

In this same year the Deutscher Werkbund, the most influential art society in Europe, held the spectacular "Film und Foto" exhibition in Stuttgart. More than a thousand photographs were hung in the thirteen galleries of the city's exposition hall. International in scope, it included photographs from America collected by Edward Weston and Edward Steichen, from Russia by El Lissitzky, from Holland by Piet Zwart, from Switzerland by Siegfried Giedion, from Germany by Moholy-Nagy. Many of the photographs were published by Franz Roh and Jan Tschichold in the book *Foto-Auge — l'oeil de photo — Photo-Eye*, with a trilingual text.

It was in this stimulating climate that Herbert Bayer became interested in photography. After apprenticeship in architectural and design firms in Linz,

Austria, and Darmstadt, Germany, he enrolled in the Bauhaus in 1921, planning to concentrate on graphic design. Although there were a lithographic press and other facilities for making fine prints, there was no course. He entered the wall-painting workshop of Wassily Kandinsky, and also began working with type. In 1923 he left the school for travel in Italy — typical *wanderjahren*, absorbing the environment, maintaining himself by house painting. On his return to Germany in 1925, he was invited by Walter Gropius, the founder of the Bauhaus, to join the faculty as a master and teach a new course in typography and advertising art.

To describe the Bauhaus esthetic as "functional" is perhaps an oversimplification, yet it was a driving force in the educational program so brilliantly directed by Walter Gropius, Lyonel Feininger, Paul Klee, Wassily Kandinsky, Josef Albers, Laszlo Moholy-Nagy and the other masters of that extraordinary school. To discover the properties of materials and the simplest and most direct way to use them was a main goal. Bayer's interest in typography and poster design fitted into this esthetic philosophy. Typography is mechanical, it is functional, it is direct; above all it is a medium of communication. For, to quote Bayer, "The Bauhaus was not interested in l'art pour l'art, but put their ideas in the service of concrete communication."

Sawmill, 1929

Bayer championed the simplest approach with the complete elimination of ornament, so that the letter forms themselves and their placement on the page became the elements of design. He advocated and still practices the entire elimination of capital letters. In Germany this was a yet more radical concept than elsewhere, for by tradition all German nouns are capitalized, and to ignore this is to "misspell." He pointed out the great saving that the universal adoption of eliminating upper case letters would bring about in the

simplification of typewriters and typesetting machines. He designed a new typeface, based on the minimum number of strokes required to recognize each character. This was not mere theory: a Bayer face was cast by the Berthold type foundry in a variety of point sizes and weights, and made commercially available.

From typography to photography was, Bayer states, a logical step. "Just as typography is human speech translated into what can be read, so photography is the translation of reality into a readable image."

He solved certain problems of pictorial poster design by using photography. Too personal an expression, too personal a style, tended to subdue the image and weaken its impact, so that a poster for chocolate became the same as one for shaving soap. He appreciated the objective character of the photograph. "Photography presents above all a document," he maintains. "It was false to overlook the new possibilities. We must *adopt* it, and put it to work, like pigment and brush. The control is not in the manipulation of the brush, but in the complete technical realization of what is seen."

Bayer's interest in photography over the years has taken three forms: camera pictures of the environment, seen from fresh viewpoints; camera records of extraordinary three-dimensional assemblages; and photomontages.

Most of the photographs taken by Bayer in the 1920s reflect the atmosphere of the Bauhaus; they are akin to the work of Moholy-Nagy, but with a somewhat stronger sense of linear design. Views looking down, especially from the Transporter Bridge in Marseilles, were a favorite subject for the Bauhaus artists. Textures: a lumber pile, his own foot against beach pebbles. And details: the soles of his mountain boots, a leg, spoons. Shadows. Negative prints. To judge from their titles, most of the twenty-six photographs he showed at the 1929 Stuttgart exhibition are in the present exhibition.

A second interest is the use of the camera to produce what Bayer calls *Fotoplastiken*. These are objects assembled for the camera: bones, geometrical models, rope, small objects placed against a textured wall or on a flat plate to create a sense of deep, infinite space. Many of the *Fotoplastiken* resemble his paintings of the 1930s. They relate in conception to the cover he designed for the 1927 Bauhaus magazine, when he set himself the problem of expressing without words the content of the periodical. His solution was to create a still life of the folded magazine itself on which he placed a drafting triangle, a pencil, a cube, a sphere and a cone. "This montage, that is the 'assemblage' of differed elements, takes place wholly *before* photographing," Bayer explains. "It is an entirely different process than photomontage, where the single photo is reduced to a part of the whole."

Bayer's photomontages, made for the most part in Berlin after he left the Bauhaus in 1928, are far more subjective than his photographs. They are charged with meaning, often humorous, and approach surrealism in their fantasy. Against a facade, outstretched hands, embedded in the palm of each an eye. A self-portrait, holding in one hand a detached section of his raised arm, as if the body was that of a manikin. A hand on a door handle, behind a nude woman: title, "Good Night, Marie." An empty picture frame, suspended against a moonlit sea: "A View of Life."

These photomontages, which have no words, lead directly to Bayer's most prolific work: posters, advertisements, magazine covers in which words and images both play equal parts. Now and again his own photographs appear in them, but always related to the words. Bayer calls this "typo-foto" production.

Cover, Bauhaus Magazine, 1928

Bayer's wide accomplishments, his varied interests, his ceaseless curiosity, have always included photography — as a means rather than as an end. His photographs, his photomontages cannot be isolated from his life work. He has made use of them as he has made use of the photographs of countless others, in his deep concern for what, for lack of a better phrase, is now called "visual communication."

Throughout his entire artistic career Bayer has been a painter as well as architect, exhibition designer, graphic designer, typographer, photographer. His views on the relation of photography to painting are therefore most pertinent. He told the members of the German Photographic Society in 1969, "While in recent times painting has been turning inward to the personal and intellectual, photography on the other hand is immediately understandable and universal. Certainly there were great painters whose discoveries and whose work have enriched our lives. In competent hands, painting is most strongly expressive. But in photography lies the value of directness. It carries within itself the kernel of a folk art of our technological age. A painting is always an abstraction, which creates on the canvas an image perceived or imagined. A photograph, because of its actuality, begins with the end product: the selection is made on the way. I can summarize this comparison between painting and photography if I say that both art forms are most convincing and effective when they are true to their unique qualities. It is therefore unnecessary to answer the question: will photography, as the greatest visual art of our time, replace painting?"

beaumont newhall

All quotations are translated from Herbert Bayer's unpublished speech to the German Photographic Society in Cologne, 1969, on the occasion of receiving its highest award, the Culture Prize.

photographs

1
Morning in Paris
1925
11⅝ x 8⅛ in.
29.5 x 20.6 cm.

2
Milan, Piazza del Duomo
1928
11⅞ x 7½ in.
30.1 x 19.0 cm.

3
Milan, Piazza del Duomo
1928
7½ x 11⅞ in.
19.0 x 30.1 cm.

4
Pont Transbordeur,
over Marseilles
1928
7½ x 11¾ in.
19.0 x 29.8 cm.

5
View from Pont Transbordeur
1928
14⅜ x 9¼ in.
36.5 x 23.6 cm.
Lent by the Museum of Modern Art
David H. McAlpin Fund

6
Old Marseilles
1928
11⅞ x 7½ in.
30.1 x 19.0 cm.

7
*Small Harbor, Marseilles**
1928
14½ x 9 in.
36.8 x 22.9 cm.

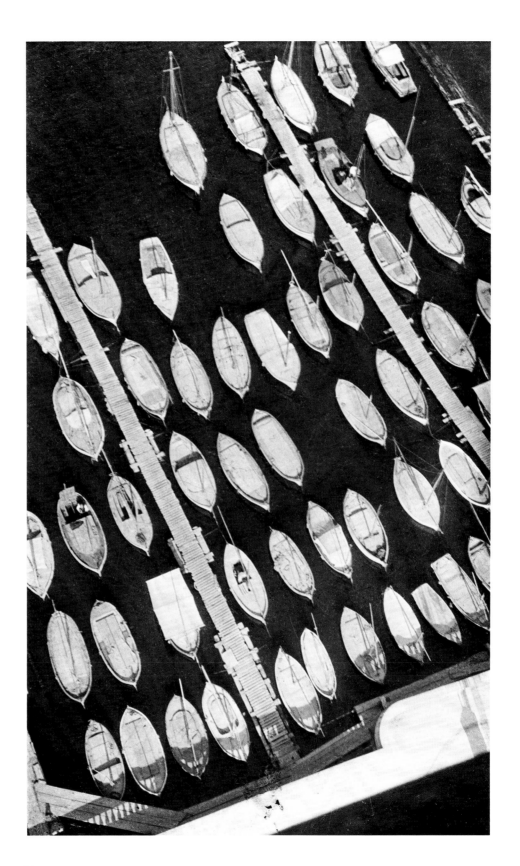

8
Marseilles, Pont
Transbordeur,
1928
11¼ x 7½ in.
28.6 x 19.0 cm.

9
Pont Transbordeur
1928
7⅜ x 11½ in.
18.7 x 29.2 cm.

10
*Pont Transbordeur**
1928
9¾ x 6⅝ in.
24.8 x 16.8 cm.

11
Shadow on Steps
1928
11⅝ x 7½ in.
29.5 x 19.0 cm.

12
Siesta*
1934
6½ x 9 in.
16.5 x 22.8 cm.

13
In France
1928
12½ x 8 in.
31.8 x 20.3 cm.

14
*Sundeck**
1928
8 x 11⅜ in.
20.3 x 28.9 cm.
Lent by the Museum of
Modern Art
David H. McAlpin Fund

15
*Self-Portrait in Mirror**
Ca. 1928
8¼ x 11⅛ in.
21.0 x 28.3 cm.

16
On the Beach*
1928
8⅞ x 5¾ in.
22.5 x 14.6 cm.

17
*Legs in Sand**
1928
14⅜ x 9⅜ in.
36.5 x 23.8 cm.

20
Pebble Beach
(Negative image)
1928
11¼ x 9 in.
22.9 x 17.1 cm.

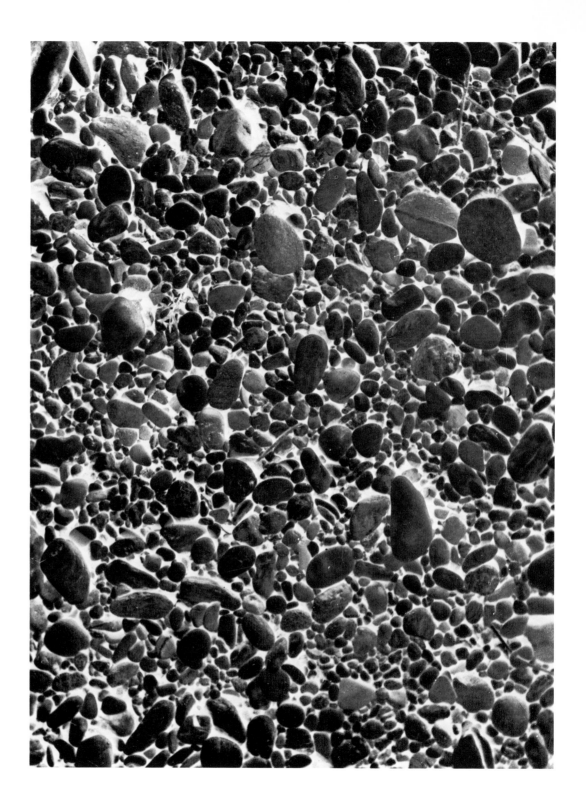

21
Pebble Beach
(Positive image)

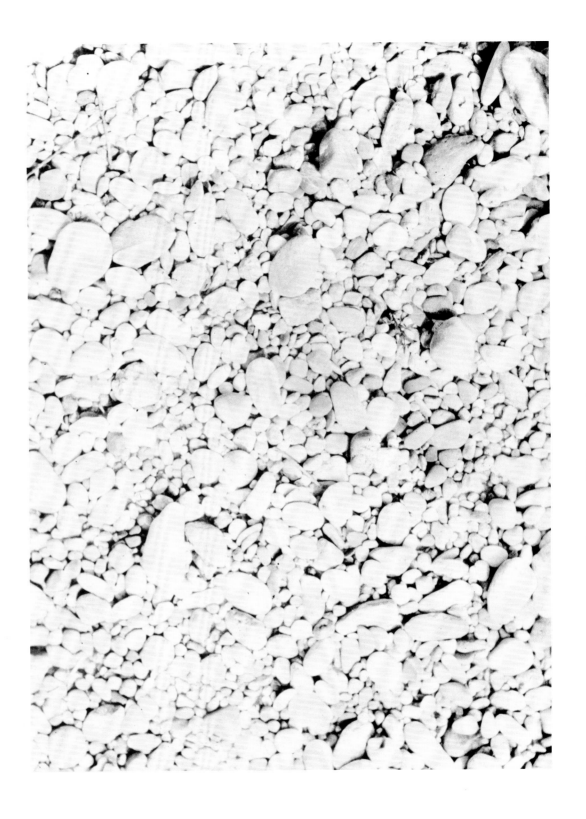

22
Pottery
1928
11⅞ x 7⅝ in.
30.2 x 19.4 cm.

23
Garden Restaurant
Ca. 1929
7⅝ x 12 in.
19.4 x 30.5 cm.

18
Flea Market
1928
9 x 6¾ in.
22.9 x 17.1 cm.

19
*Boccia**
1928
5⅜ x 8½ in.
13.6 x 21.6 cm.

24
Wannsee Beach, Berlin
1929
8¼ x 11⅞ in.
21.0 x 30.1 cm.

25
Glass Eyes
1929
11⅝ x 8 in.
29.6 x 20.3 cm.

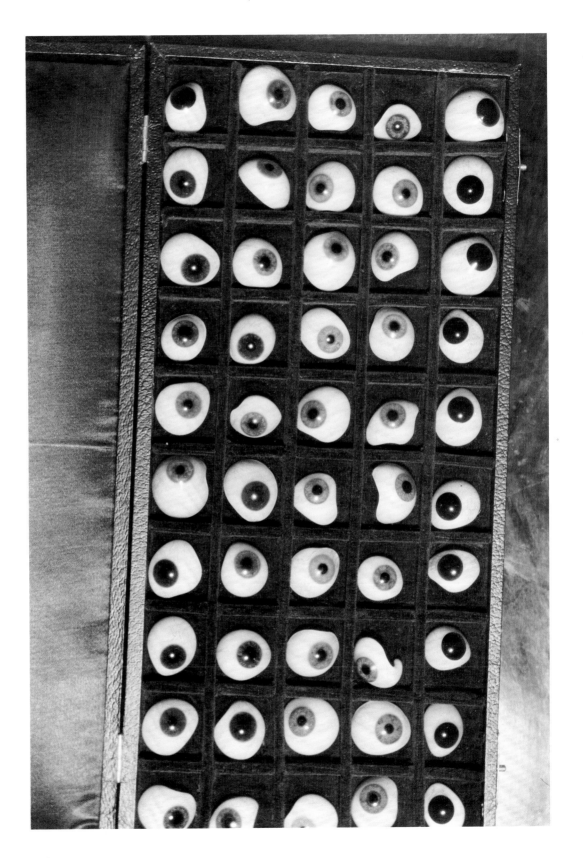

26
Ascona
1929
12⅛ x 8⅜ in.
30.8 x 21.3 cm.

27
Castello Sforza
Ca. 1930
11½ x 7⅝ in.
29.2 x 19.4 cm.

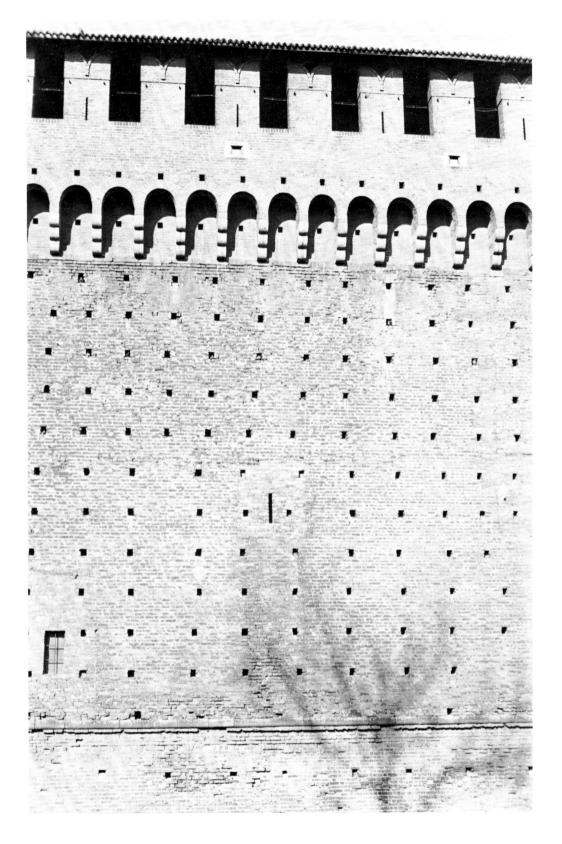

28
*Playing Knight**
1930
8⅞ x 11¼ in.
22.5 x 28.6 cm.

29
Smoking Knight
1930
11¼ x 8⅛ in.
28.6 x 20.6 cm.

30
*Double Image**
1930
8⅜ x 11 in.
21.3 x 28.0 cm.

31
Knight with Flower*
1930
9¼ x 11⅝ in.
23.5 x 29.6 cm.

32
Gothic
(Negative image)
1931
8½ x 11⅜ in.
21.6 x 28.9 cm.

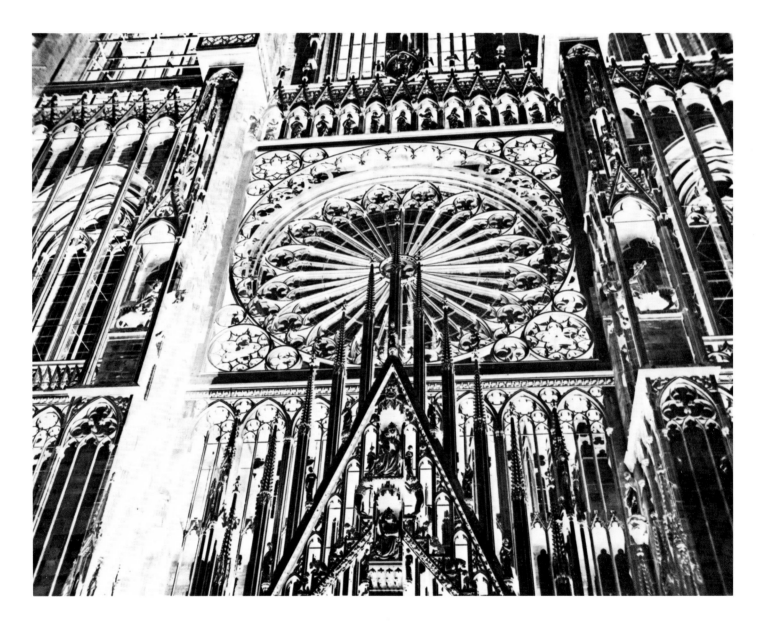

33
Gothic
(Positive image)

34
Posters in Athens
1934
10⅛ x 9½ in.
25.7 x 24.1 cm.

35
Street Cafe, Greece
1934
9⅞ x 9⅜ in.
25.1 x 23.8 cm.

36
Beggar in Serbia
1934
8⅛ x 11¾ in.
20.6 x 29.8 cm.

37
At the Acropolis
1934
8⅛ x 11¾ in.
20.6 x 29.8 cm.

38
Volcano
1934
10 x 9⅜ in.
25.4 x 24.1 cm.

39
Midday
1934
10 x 9½ in.
25.4 x 24.1 cm.

40
Parapoatiani Chapel,
Mykonos
1934
7 x 11¼ in.
17.8 x 28.5 cm.

41
Stairs to Santorin
1934
10 × 9½ in.
25.4 × 24.2 cm.

42
Fishing Boat
1934
7⅜ x 11¾ in.
19.7 x 29.8 cm.

43
Fishing in Corfu
1934
10 x 9½ in.
25.4 x 24.1 cm.

44
Olive Grove
1934
10 x 9½ in.
25.4 x 24.1 cm.

45
Old Olive Trees
1934
10 x 9½ in.
25.4 x 24.1 cm.

46
Good Morning
Ca. 1936
7½ x 11½ in.
19.1 x 29.2 cm.

47
House of My Childhood
Date unknown
10 x 9⅞ in.
25.4 x 25.1 cm.

48
In Austria
Ca. 1933
7⅞ x 11⅜ in.
20.0 x 28.9 cm.

49
Spoon Sale*
1936
8⅜ x 11 in.
22.2 x 27.9 cm.

50
My Climbing Boots
1936
9¾ x 8½ in.
24.7 x 21.6 cm.

51
Self-Portrait
1937
6 x 7¼ in.
15.3 x 18.4 cm.

52
*Shells**
Date unknown
11⅝ x 15¼ in.
29.5 x 38.5 cm.

53
*Shells**
Date unknown
$11^{5}/_{8}$ x $15^{1}/_{2}$ in.
29.5 x 39.4 cm.

photomontages

Profil en Face
1929
13¼ x 10⅝ in.
33.7 x 27.0 cm.

55
Bone Breaker
1931
15⅞ x 11¾ in.
40.3 x 29.8 cm.

56
Look into Life
1931
14 x 11½ in.
35.6 x 29.2 cm.

57
The Language of Letters
1931
14⅝ x 11⅝ in.
37.1 x 29.5 cm.

58
The Kiss
1932
13½ x 10 in.
34.3 x 25.4 cm.

60
Among Odalisques
Ca. 1931
16 x 12 in.
40.6 x 30.5 cm.

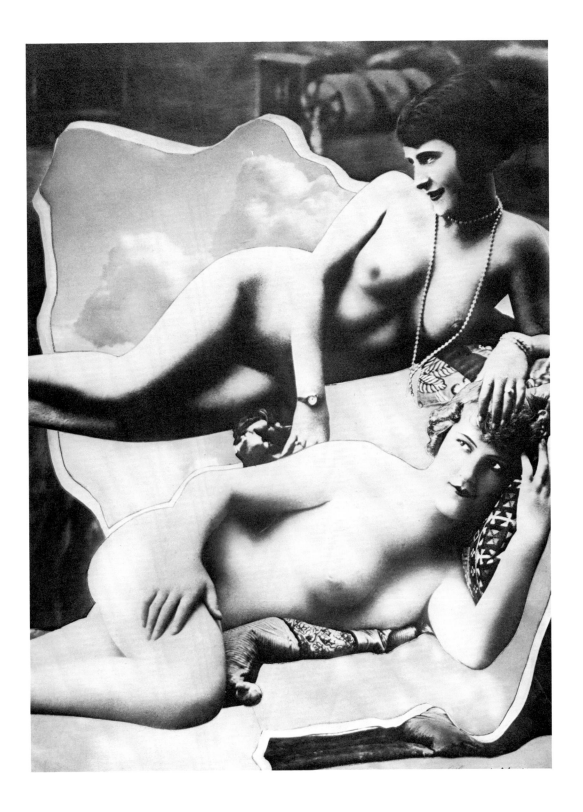

61
Creation
1932
15 x 9½ in.
38.1 x 24.1 cm.

62
Lonely Metropolitan
1932
13⅜ x 10½ in.
34.0 x 26.6 cm.

63
Monument
1932
13¼ x 8 in.
33.6 x 20.3 cm.

64
Self-Portrait
1932
15 x 11½ in.
38.1 x 29.2 cm.

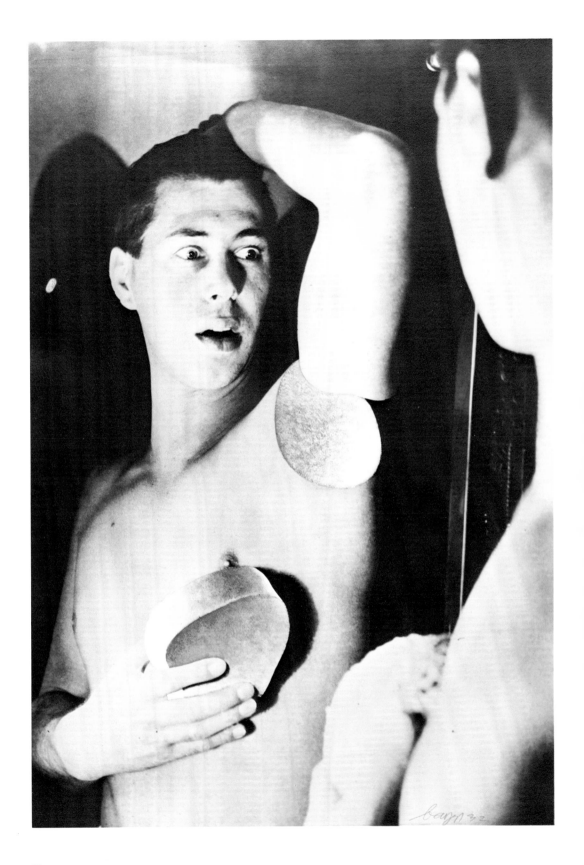

fotoplastiken

65
Hands Act
1932
15 x 11 in.
38.1 x 27.9 cm.

66
Nature Morte
1936
10½ x 12¾ in.
26.6 x 32.4 cm.

67
Metamorphosis
1936
10⅛ x 13⅜ in.
25.7 x 34.0 cm.

68
Bones with Sea
1936
9⅜ x 12 in.
23.8 x 30.5 cm.

69
Shortly before Dawn
1936
11 x 15½ in.
27.9 x 39.4 cm.

70
Stable Wall
1936
10¾ x 15¼ in.
27.3 x 38.7 cm.

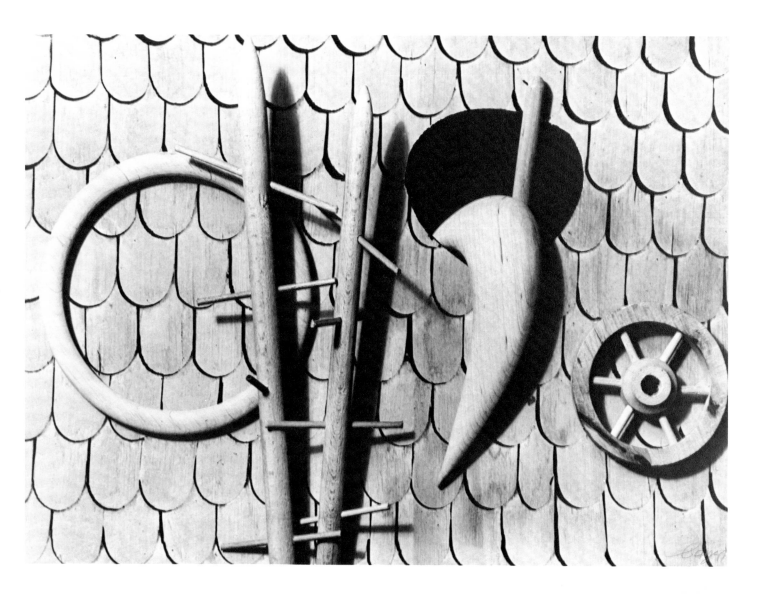

71
Wall with Shingles
1936
11 x 15 in.
28.0 x 38.1 cm.

72
Winter
1936
11⅛ x 14¾ in.
28.3 x 37.5 cm.

73
Still Life
1936
10¾ x 15½ in.
27.3 x 39.3 cm.

74
Standing Objects
1936
15¼ x 10⅜ in.
38.8 x 26.4 cm.

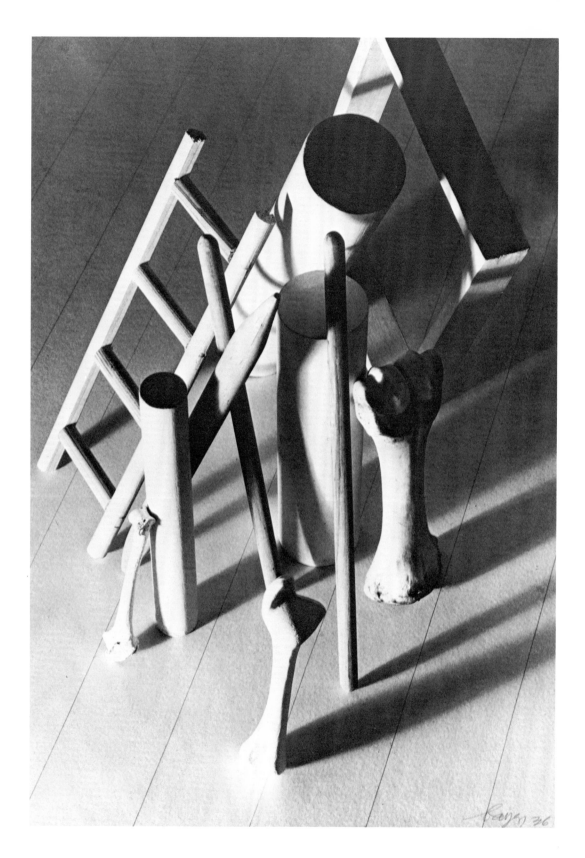

Books

Ades, Dawn. *Photomontage.* New York:
Pantheon Books, 1976.

Bayer, Herbert; Gropius, Walter;
Gropius, Ise, eds. *Bauhaus 1919-1928.*
New York: The Museum of Modern Art,
1938, bibliography.

————. *Herbert Bayer: Painter, Designer,
Architect.* New York: Reinhold Book
Division, 1967, autobiography, bibliography.

Dorner, Alexander. *The Way Beyond Art;
The Work of Herbert Bayer.* New York:
Wittenborn and Schulz, Inc., 1947.

Rotzler, W. *Photography as Artistic
Experiment: From Fox Talbot to
Moholy-Nagy.* New York: American
Photographic Book Publishing Co., Inc.,
1976.

Wescher, Herta. *Collage.* Translated by
Robert E. Wolf. New York: Harry N. Abrams,
Inc., 1968.

Articles

Bayer, Herbert. "Aus dem Optischen
Notizbuch." *Das Illustrierte Blatt,* No. 5,
1928.

————. "Die Schwebefähre von Marseille."
Das Illustrierte Blatt, No. 49, 1929.

————. "Werbephoto." *Wirtschaftlichkeit*
February 1928.

Frenzel, H. K. "Herbert Bayer."
Gebrauchsgraphik, May 1931, pp. 2-19.

Hirschfeld, Kurt. "Die Moderne
Photographie." *Gebrauchsgraphik,* July
1930, pp. 44-51.

Hölscher, Eberhard. "Herbert Bayer."
Gebrauchsgraphik, 1935, pp. 13-15.

————. "Herbert Bayer."
Gebrauchsgraphik, 1936, pp. 18-25.

————. "Herbert Bayer."
Gebrauchsgraphik, 1938, pp. 2-16.

Jay, Bill, ed. "Herbert Bayer of the
Bauhaus." *Creative Camera,* November
1968, p. 404.

Levy, Julien. "From a Portfolio of
Photomontages by Herbert Bayer."
Coronet, January 1940, pp. 30-37.

Lohse, Bernd. "Photo-journalism: The
Legendary Twenties." *Camera,* April 1967,
pp. 5-23.

Moholy-Nagy, Laszlo. "From the Bauhaus."
Camera, April 1967, pp. 24-35.

Neumann, Eckhard. "Herbert Bayer's
Photographic Experiments."
Typographica II, 1965, pp. 34-44.

Porter, Allan, ed. "Photography — A
Contemporary Compendium: Biographies."
Camera, November 1975, pp. 14, 40.

Steinorth, Karl. "Herbert Bayer (1900)."
Color (Germany), October 1975, pp. 36-37.

Westheim, Paul. "Herbert Bayer,
Photograph und Maler." *Das Kunstblatt,*
1929, pp. 151-153.

Catalogs

Linz, Wolfgang-Gurlitt Museum.
"Herbert Bayer: Beispiele aus dem
Gesamtwerk, 1919-1974." Peter Baum,
1976.

London, Marlborough Fine Art Ltd.
"Herbert Bayer." Introduction by
Ludwig Grote, 1968.

Munich, Galerie Klihm. "Fotoauge
Herbert Bayer." Introduction by
Eckhard Neumann (no date).

Vienna, Foto Galerie die Brücke. Exhibition
announcement: letter in English from
Herbert Bayer with chronology, 1971.

The contemporary prints were printed by
Michaela Murphy, International Museum of
Photography at George Eastman House.
Frontispiece photographed by Phil Kirkley,
Atlantic Richfield Company.

The catalog was designed in Los Angeles
by Lilli Cristin in cooperation with
Herbert Bayer. 2,500 copies were printed
on Quintessence by Precision Graphics.

Photo on page 9 courtesy of
International Museum of Photography
at George Eastman House.